MINI COLOR SERIES

LEOPARD 2A5

Text & Photos by Walter Böhm
Illustrations by Hubert Cance

ISBN962-361-637-6
printed in Hong Kong

Leopard 2 battle tanks form the backbone of NATO's armored units. Mobility, firepower and armor protection are balanced together to the optimum in this weapons system, and it shows in their records of high reliability and operating safety. Because of the outstanding results achieved by the tank's powerful 120mm gun, the Leopard 2 teams have won foremost recognition in many of NATO's international competitions, such as the Canadian Army Trophy (CAT). The Leopard 2 weapons system has now been in use for 15 years in the tank and tank reconnaissance units of the German Army, as well as among other NATO partners.

The development of the Leopard 2 was initiated in 1969 with the end of the governmental agreement between the Federal Republic of Germany and the USA on the joint "Battle Tank 70" project. The developmental aims, which were set very high at that time, could not be realized because of the costs, which had exceeded DM 830 million. The increasing financial requirements forced the joint German/American "Tank 70/Main Battle Tank 70" project to be abandoned. Both countries now concentrated their efforts on the development of their own national projects. The USA built the XM-1 and Germany concentrated on the further development of the Leopard 1.

At the beginning of 1970 the German Army decided to develop a completely new type of tank, the "Leopard 2", based on the experimental development of the "Golden Leopard" that was continued along with the joint "Kpz 70" project. Kraus-Maffei in Munich was selected as the general contractor for the development of the new Leopard 2 battle tank because of their experience in constructing the Leopard 1. In the next few years 17 prototype turrets fitted with 105mm and 120mm guns from Rheinmetall were made, as well as 16 chassis. The company delivered the first prototypes of the Leopard 2K battle tank from 1972 to 1973.

The Yom Kippur war of 1973 brought about a new way of thinking in the business of tank construction. The evaluation of the knowledge gained from the Israeli-Egyptian war showed that tank protection was more valuable than previously assumed. As a result, the Leopard 2 was fitted with a new turret with more protection. In the middle of the 1970s there were extensive trials and comparisons made in Germany and in the USA. Two Leopard 2 battle tanks were flown to the USA where a series of comparisons were made with the XM-1. The advantages of the Leopard 2 were clearly shown. (The 105mm gun had already been exchanged for a more powerful 120mm gun in America.) Another goal of the exercises in the USA was to decide on a joint standard of components for both battle tanks, but nothing more than an agreement to install the 120mm gun in both the M1 and the Leopard 2 was achieved.

With the purchase of the weapons system approved by the German Ministry of Defense, the Leopard 2 was officially presented to the German public in 1977. At the end of 1979 the first standard Leopard 2 tanks were delivered to Panzerlehrbrigade 9 in Münster. The Leopard 2 of the first batch had no thermal imaging device, but it was installed in the second batch as standard equipment. At this time the second manufacturer of the Leopard 2, MAK in Kiel, was still experimenting and making adjustments in the tank construction between the USA and Germany. The installation of the M1 gas turbine AGT 1500X 1100A in the Leopard 2 tank was stopped because of the high cost. Between 1979 and 1992, a total of 2,125 Leopard 2 battle tanks, as well as 75 armored recovery vehicles — the Bergepanzer 3 "Büffel" (based on the Leopard 2 chassis) — were manufactured in 8 Baulos (batches) by Kraus-Maffei in Munich and Krupp MAK in Kiel.

The German Army designated the Leopard 2 of the second and third batches as the "A1", and refitted vehicles from the first batch are the "A2". Vehicles fitted with the new SEM 80/90 radio are known as Leopard 2A3. The German Army calls those from the fifth batch the Leopard 2A4.

Gebirgspanzerbatallion 8 received the last delivery of Leopard 2A4s from the 8th batch. During the production of the entire eight batches, alterations and refits were made. The aim of the German Army was to bring all of the Leopard 2 battle tanks up to the same equipment standard. Most of the Leopard 2 tanks of the German Army are the A4.

Leopard 2A5 KWS (Increased Battle Ability)

With the goal of maintaining superiority on the battlefield in the future, the "Leopard User Club" agreed to develop increased battle ability. The principal features of the KWS are improved armor protection in the turret area, as well as increased night-fighting ability and driving ability while firing on the move in battle. This type is also called the "Mannheimer Configuration".

In 1992 the German Army decided to refit 225 of their Leopard 2 fleet to the A5 standard, and to equip their tank battalions for reacting to difficult crises. The chassis of batches 6, 7 and 8 were refitted for this purpose, as were the old turrets of batches 1, 2 and 3. The armor protection on the front of the turret and the turret sides was reinforced with the spare parts of the outer module of the 4th generation technology, which can resist several hits by KE (Kinetic Energy) ammunition and hollow charged shells. However, the tank's battle weight is inevitably increased by this from 55 tonnes to 62.5 tonnes.

KE APFSDS-T ammunition with no casing, as well as multi-purpose HEAT-MPT can be fired from the Leopard 2's proven 120mm gun. The APFSDS-T shells can penetrate the hardest tank alloys and melt the tank steel while penetrating it. Also, two 7.62mm machine guns are provided for self-defense. Thanks to a more powerful, fully electronic, weapons-loading system (necessary because of the heavy turret weight), the Leopard 2A5 keeps its target in its sights even at full speed over rough ground. The digital computer of the gunner's EMES-15 stabilized fire-control computer calculates the speed of the target by laser beam in fractions of a second. In connection with the weapons-loading system, the initial hit probability in combat at a distance of 2,500 meters (2,732 yards) is over 80%.

Another principal item in the KWS is the increased poor-weather and night-fighting ability. The Leopard 2A5 commander observes, controls and fights with the use of his PERI-R 17A2 periscope with integrated thermal imaging device, at night and in poor weather, independent of the gunner's thermal imaging device. The tank commander can perform panoramic reconnaissance, but the gunner takes his aim independent of this, so the hunter-killer function is also ensured at night. The commander can still supervise and control his gunner by transferring the data of the gunner to his own monitor. The driver of the Leopard 2A5 has a driver's low-light-level appliance and can also see and drive backwards with the help of a video monitor. The hydraulic gears have four forward and two reverse gears, and the 1,500 HP, 12-cylinder MTU MB 873 diesel engine can accelerate the Leopard 2 up to 75 km/h (46.5 mph). In a 100-kilometer street march, the Leopard 2 uses 215 liters (134 gallons) of diesel fuel. The Leopard 2's range of action is 550 kilometers (342 miles), and three-meter (9 feet) wide trenches and 1.10-meter (3.5 feet) high walls are no hindrance to the tank's cross-country abilities. The DM 8.5 million Leopard 2A5 KWS is the most modern and powerful battle tank in the world today.

Euro-Leopard 2

The Netherlands was the first NATO member to put Leopard 2 battle tanks— 445 altogether — into service between 1982 and 1986. The Dutch Army also sold 114 Leopard 2A4 tanks to Austria in 1997. Of the remaining Leopard 2A4 battle tanks, 180 vehicles will initially be refitted to the Leopard 2A5 standard. It is planned that the rest will eventually become KWS vehicles also. The Dutch Army still has 25 Bergepanzer 3 Büffel armored recovery vehicles.

In 1984, following extensive comparison tests with the American M1, neutral Switzerland also decided to introduce 380 Leopard 2 battle tanks into its arsenal. They will mainly be built in Switzerland under license and will be called "Leopard Tank 87".

At the beginning of 1990 the British Army also showed interest in the Leopard battle tank as a replacement for the Challenger 1. In comparison tests in Great Britain, the Leopard 2 took first place ahead of the American Abrams M1 and the Challenger 2, but the Challenger will be given priority for political reasons (employment opportunities).

In troop trials in Sweden in 1994 the Leopard 2 fulfilled the demands made on it, surpassing both the Abrams M1 and the French LeClerc. Then Sweden leased 160 Strv 121 "Leopard 2A4" from the German Army for 15 years. One hundred twenty new Strv 122 "Leopard 2A5" will be manufactured, and another 90 Strv 122 "Leopard 2A5" and 17 Büffel armored recovery vehicles are planned. There will be some further improvements made on the Swedish Strv 122 "Leopard 2A5" (compared to the German/Dutch versions) such as: extra armor on the chassis (Spall Liners), extra armor on the turret roof, modular tank command and control system (TCCS), as well as safe-for-the-eye lasers (RAMAN lasers).

In 1995/96 Spain rented 108 Leopard 2A4 battle tanks from stocks of the German Army for equipping their heavy Eurocorps units. Another 219 Leopard 2A5 vehicles are to be built under license. Austria has purchased 114 Leopard 2A4 NL from the Dutch forces, in the course of Holland's arms reduction, and will refit their tank battalion with these, which are presently equipped with the old M60A3. Denmark has also shown interest in taking over used Leopard 2 tanks from the German Army. Based on their positive experience with the Leopard 1 battle tank, the future adoption of the Leopard 2 weapons system is likely.

Summary

The Leopard 2 battle tank has been introduced into six European countries, and the 120mm smoothbore gun of the Leopard 2 has been installed in the American Abrams M1A1 tank. Testing is being carried out to increase the firepower through lengthening the previous barrel of the 120mm smoothbore gun from a caliber length of L/44 to L/55 by 1.30 meters (4.3 feet) and providing the crews with improved ammunition. So far no use has been made of the increase in the engine output. The final stage in the development of the Leopard 2 should be the fitting of a 140mm battle tank gun, along with the issuance of special ammunition for fighting helicopters. From the manufacture of the first standard vehicles in 1979 until today, the Leopard 2 has been continually maintained in the latest technical condition. With the increasing demand for the main weapons system for many battle tank units of NATO and non-NATO countries, it should remain so for the foreseeable future.

Thanks are extended to the Panzerbrigade 12 "Oberpfalz", Oberstleutnant Schäfer and Hauptmann Joos, the Panzerbatallion 33, Oberleutenant Bruns, as well as Andreas Kirchhoff, Egon Merk, Roland Hochstatter, Wolfgang Langwucht, Herbert Hept and Peter Blume.

Abbreviations
PzBtl = Panzerbataillon (Tank battalion)
PzLBtl= Panzerlehrbataillon (Tank training battalion)
GebPzBtl= Gebirgspanzerbataillon (Mountain tank battalion)

Shoulder badge of 5 (GE) Panzerdivision.

Shoulder badge of 7 (GE) Panzerdivision.

Shoulder badge of 10 (GE) Panzerdivision.

Shoulder badge of Kampftruppenschule (combat troop school), the training unit of the German Army tank, reconnaissance and mechanized infantry.

ORGANIZATION CHART: BATTALION (ORGABAT)

Panzerbataillon (armored battalion)
(Army Structure 5)

1st Company – HHC (Headquarters/Headquarters Company)

-Battalion command group	1x Leopard of Battalion command
-Company command squad	
-Signal section	2x M113 command post
-Scout/Recce platoon	6x Wolf ATV, 16x Krad motorbike
-Ambulance platoon	
-Logistics platoon	
-Maintenance platoon	4x Bergepanzer 3 Büffel ARV

2nd, 3rd, 4th, 5th Armored Company each with

-Company command squad	1x Wolf, 1x Leopard 2, 2x truck
-Four platoons	13x Leopard 2

Crew, Mobility and Firepower of the Leopard 2 Battle Tank

The Federal Republic of Germany and the USA parted ways after the "Battle Tank 70" project was cancelled. The USA then built the M1 Abrams battle tank, and Germany began developing a completely new tank, the "Leopard 2". The first M1 Abrams standard vehicles were fitted with the 105mm gun. Later the German 120mm Rheinmetall gun of the Leopard 2 battle tank would be installed on the M1A1 version of the Abrams. This photo shows an M1 of the 2nd US Cavalry Regiment and a Leopard 2A4 (5th batch) tank of Panzerbatallion 293 during "Reforger 88" maneuvers. (W. Langwucht).

The crew of the Leopard 2 consists of four tankers: tank commander, driver, gunner, and assistant gunner. The tank commander is responsible for the vehicle, gives orders regarding the direction and speed to the driver, and controls firepower in battle. The driver drives the heavy, 55-tonne Leopard 2 battle tank on the instructions of the commander. The gunner is responsible for firing the tank's 120mm gun under direction of the commander. The fourth member of the crew is the assistant gunner who loads the 120mm gun with cartridges weighing between 19 and 23 kg (42 and 50 lb.). He is also responsible for operating the anti-aircraft machine gun on the turret. The Leopard 2 fires KE munitions (KE = kinetic energy impact projectile with initial high speed) from the 120mm L/44 smoothbore gun, which is called the APFSDS-T, seen at left in this photo. At right is the MZ munitions (MZ = All-purpose hollow charged and detonation shells with a low starting speed), also known as HEAT-MP, which can be used against all targets, including bunkers. The cartridges are fired without casings.

Central Europe is threaded with many rivers and lakes. The Leopard 2 can cross lakes of one meter (3.3 feet) in depth. By attaching supplementary equipment, such as that seen on this Leopard of Panzerbataillon 4/63, this depth can be increased to 2.35 meters (7.7 feet).

A Leopard 2 battle tank of 4th Company of Panzerbataillon 63 is fitted with a special snorkel. Using this snorkel it is possible to drive underwater down to a depth of 4 meters (13 feet).

A Leopard 2 of Panzerbataillon 2/143 is shown here at the railway station at Hoya in October 1990. During troop training exercises the Leopard 2 tank battalions of the German Army are moved by rail. The German Army either uses their own rail cars for this or they rent them from German Railways. Because of the extra-wide load of the Leopard 2, the heavy front track aprons are tipped up during rail transport. From the fifth batch on, the munitions hatch on the left side of the turret was reinforced and welded shut to increase the resistance of the turret.

Emblem of Panzerbataillon 143, Panzerbrigade 14, 5 (GE) Panzerdivision.

The cross-country ability of the Leopard 2 is impressive. The tank chassis has a ground clearance of 540 mm (1.7 feet), so the vehicle can climb a wall that is 1.10 meter (3.6 feet) high and has the ability to cross a 3 meter (9.8 feet) wide trench. The 1,500 HP diesel engine provides the Leopard 2 with the necessary mobility on the field of battle.

The 55-tonne Leopard 2 battle tank is powered by a turbo, water-cooled, 12-cylinder MTU MB 873 diesel engine that provides 1,500 HP at 2,600 revs, giving a power/weight ratio of 27 HP per ton. The power/weight ratio for a "Battle Tank 70" is 32.8 HP per metric ton.

A Leopard 2 of Panzerbataillon 123 during the "Frommer Schweppermann 93" maneuver on the troop training ground of the US 7th Army at Hohenfels. The chassis of the Leopard 2, which is mounted on a torsion bar suspension, has a good record for safe operation.

Details of the Leopard 2 turret. At left is the space for the assistant gunner with the MG 3 anti-aircraft gun. To the right sits the tank commander, who can operate the co-axial Blenden machine gun from his seat.

The driver steers the Leopard 2 battle tank with a servomechanism in the form of a steering knob, so that the tank is easier to steer than a car. The power changeable planetary switch gears, with four forward and two reverse gears, are switched by an automatic gearshift.

At a fighting distance of 2,500 meters (2,732.5 yards), the hit ratio of the Leopard 2 is over 80%. A maximum fighting distance of 4 kilometers (2.5 miles), with deviations, is possible. The Leopard 2 has a stock of munitions of 42 projectiles, 15 of which are stored in the turret.

Origin and Meaning of the Insignia of the Leopard 2 Battalions of Panzerbrigade 12 "Oberpfalz" (as at October 1990)

It was customary for the Leopard 2 tank battalions of the German Army to put their battalion insignia on the front of the turret. The insignia of the Leopard 2 tank battalions of Panzerbrigade 12 was in yellow. Panzerbataillon 121 had a sword in a triangle for their insignia. The sword is double-edged, which is supposed to emphasize their status as a combat unit and show that two edges — tank and tank grenadier — are needed for proper operation.

Insignia of Panzerbataillon 123, Panzerbrigade 12, painted at the front of the Leopard 2 turret. The insignia of PzBtl 123 shows the "Knight Helmet" of Seyfried Schweppermann who lived in the 14th century.

The yellow knight's helmet is the special symbol of the Panzerbataillon 123, the second Leopard 2 tank battalion of Panzerbrigade 12, that was applied to every vehicle of the unit. The helmet was originally worn by the armies of knights in the 14th century. Symbolizing the hard-hitting power of highly mobile troops, the helmet is used today as an emblem by modern tank units. In 1974 the helmet was adopted as the official unit insignia of the Amberger Panzerbataillon 123.

Another Leopard 2 tank battalion of Panzerbrigade 12 was Panzerbataillon 124. In June 1969 the insignia of the unit was presented for the first time at the 10th anniversary of the formation of the battalion. In the middle of the yellow insignia there is a Y on a tank track, the sign of the heavy unit, similar to the Y emblem of the former 7.Panzerdivision in the Second World War. All three Leopard 2 tank battalions of Panzerbrigade 12 were dissolved because of the altered political situation in the world and the reduction of troops in the German Army at the beginning of the 1990s. This photo was taken at the German/Canadian exercise "Royal Sword 90".

"Charging Knight" insignia of a Panzerbataillon 33 Leopard 2 tank, painted on the front side of the turret. The yellow "Wolfsangel" is the maneuver marking at Hohenfels in January 1996.

Leopard 2A1 to A4 in Action with the German Bundeswehr

During the army exercise "Flinker Igel" in September 1984, the Leopard 2 was subjected for the first time to the burdens of large-scale maneuvers. In order to test inter-operability, Panzerbataillon 241 (consisting of a company of M1s (105mm) Abrams of 1st Battalion, 64th Armored, US 3rd Infantry Division, a company of Leopard 2s and a company of Marder personnel carriers) was formed. The logistical problems of the various types of battle tanks proved to be difficult to overcome. The M1 tank had to be supplied with other operating materials and required an additional share of supply and maintenance personnel in Panzerbataillon 241. Seen here is a Leopard 2A1 (Batch 2/3) of Panzerbataillon 241 during the "Flinker Igel 84" maneuver, painted olive-green with mud camouflage, which was normal during large maneuvers before the German Bundeswehr introduced its three-color camouflage. (E. Merk)

A Leopard 2A3 of Panzerlehrbataillon 94, Panzerlehrbrigade 9, part of the "Aggressor Force", near Soltau during the army exercise "Trutzige Sachsen 85". Beginning with batch number 4, the factories in Munich and Kiel delivered all Leopard 2 battle tanks to the German Army with the new three-color camouflage of bronze-green, leather brown and tar black. The new German three-color camouflage was then adopted by the US, French, Dutch and Swiss armies. Experience has shown that the possibility of detection with this new type of spot camouflage, compared with the previous olive-green, is reduced by more than half. Of the vehicles of the 4th batch that were designated "A3", there were altogether 300 manufactured and fitted with the new SEM 80/90 radio, as well as the shorter antenna.

The 2nd Company of Panzerbataillon 244 camouflaged their Leopard 2 a little unusually during the "Keckers Spatz" maneuver in September 1987 near Ingolstadt in southern Germany. The black spots of the three-color camouflage were partially painted over with a light mud color and camouflaged with pieces of clothes. This camouflage is similar to the old US-MERDEC camouflage of the 1980s. Just as on the tanks from the 2nd batch, the towing cable at the rear of the Leopard 2 was fitted crosswise. (W. Langwucht)

This Leopard 2A4 battle tank (5th batch), Panzerbataillon 293 of Panzerbrigade 29, is seen near Ansbach during the Reforger maneuver "Certain Challenge" in 1988. The vehicle bears the Reforger maneuver insignia of the "Blue Force" on the turret. Panzerbataillon 293 received the first Leopard 2 battle tanks in September 1986. At this time Panzerbataillon 293 was organized according to Army Structure 4, with a headquarters company and three battle companies. In 1983 Panzerbataillon 293 took part in the CAT competition, using the Leopard 1A4 at the time, and was adjudged the best tank unit in the competition. (W. Langwucht)

During the maneuvers in Germany the armored units continuously practiced rapid advances, as well as counterattacks, with the support of folding bridge systems. Here we see a Leopard 2A4 battle tank of Panzeraufklärungsbataillon 12 crossing a German version of the American-designed Ribbon Bridge of 12.Panzerdivision near Farr on the Main river. The Ribbon Bridge can support armored vehicles weighing up to 80 tonnes and can be used as either a ferry or a fixed bridge. (H. Hept)

During the Dutch maneuver "Light Viper 93", heavy reconnaissance troops of the German Army were used. A Leopard 2A4 (6th batch) of Panzeraufklärungslehrbataillon 11 of Panzerlehrbrigade 9 engaged in fighting a Dutch Leopard 2. The most apparent alteration of the 6th batch of tanks is the placement of new heavy track protection at the front of the chassis. Other innovations of the A4 version are digitized computers for extra types of ammunition, fire-control system, maintenance-free batteries, and improved armor plating on the turret and front of the chassis.

Emblem of Panzeraufklärungsbataillon 11, Panzerlehrbrigade 9, painted at the front of the Leopard 2 turret.

This Leopard 2A4 of Panzeraufklärungsbataillon 12 from "Red Training Troop", shown near Hofheim/Ebern, is fitted with the German AGDUS training system. The tank reconnaissance battalions are the eyes and ears of the division. According to the new Army Structure 5 of the German Army, the heavy tank reconnaissance battalions make up three companies that consist of Leopard 2 battle tanks and ten Luchs wheeled reconnaissance vehicles. At some future date the heavy reconnaissance companies employing the Leopard 2 are to be dissolved, leaving only those with the Luchs reconnaissance vehicle intact. (H. Hept)

The crew of 3rd Company of Panzerbataillon 84 has decorated the turret of their Leopard 2A4 with interesting camouflage. The unit is playing the part of the aggressor force during the "Light Viper 93" maneuvers.

Firing in the fog! The electronics in the Leopard 2 enables the battle tank to fire its 120mm L/44 smoothbore gun while at a standstill, when moving, or when visibility is poor. The stronger armor (no welded munitions hatch) attached to the turret of this Leopard 2A4 (6th batch) of Panzerbataillon 304 is clearly visible in this photo.

Combat training in the German Army has achieved a new high standard with the "Laser Maneuvers" of the Leopard 2 tank battalions at the US 7th Army's CMTC Hohenfels (Combat Maneuver Training Center). The soldiers learn more and learn faster with the American SAWE-RF/MILES II (Multiple Integrated Laser Engagement System) training system than with the usual maneuvers. The use of dual simulators forces them to adopt a combat type of attitude. Here a Leopard 2A4 (6th batch) of Panzerbataillon 304 of "Gold Force" (indicated by the red cross) is seen in a partially covered position during the Spring 1994 maneuvers at the CMTC. The camouflage consisting of linen material on the front part of the vehicle is typical for PzBtl 304. The crew has also spread two umbrellas over the turret hatch to protect them against the weather.

All vehicles are fitted with detector belts during the maneuvers at the CMTC Hohenfels, and the MILES sensors may not be covered or soiled. The "Gold Force" is signified by red crosses. This photo shows a Leopard 2A4 (6th batch) that features lightweight track aprons and the typical fabric camouflage of Panzerbataillon 304, 10.Panzerdivision.

There was no difference between the type A4 Leopards of batches 6 and 7, altogether 83 vehicles were manufactured by Krauss-Maffei in the 6th batch, and 67 Leopard 2 battle tanks by MAK. The 7th batch was composed of 55 vehicles made by Krauss-Maffei and 45 made by MAK. The photo shows a Leopard 2A4 (6/7th batch) of Panzerbataillon 304 at CMTC Hohenfels in April 1994.

In order to avoid damage to the chassis of the Leopard, the side aprons were removed during the exercises at CMTC Hohenfels. The suspension of the chassis on the wheels is shown to advantage here. This Leopard 2A4 of Panzerbataillon 304 has turned its main gun to "6 o'clock" after being taken out of action. The SAWE-RF/MILES II training system differentiates between four types of out-of-combat status: total, chassis, weapons systems, and radio.

A Leopard 2A4 platoon of Panzerbataillon 304 attacks during an exercise in January 1996 at the CMTC Hohenfels. The white vertical stripes of the "Zebra" winter camouflage obscures the contours of the vehicle at a distance of 2,500 meters (2,732.5 yards). The SAWE-RF/MILES II training equipment, whose yellow combat vehicle "kill" indicator recognition lights blink continually after a "hit", is clearly visible on the turret of the Leopard. In the background a Gepard anti-aircraft tank surveys the vast sky hoping to avoid any unpleasant surprises.

The 8th and last batch of Leopard 2s was manufactured between January 1991 and March 1992. Krauss-Maffei built 41 and MAK built 34 Leopard 2A4 of the final batch. The vehicles of the 8th batch can be recognized externally by the improved heavy track aprons, their continuous steel side aprons, both of which are of D technology (3 protection versions), and the field adjusting mirror on the mouth of the 120mm gun. To improve the cross-country capabilities of the Leopard, the crew has exchanged part of the rubber padding for ice scrapers that are affixed to the front of the vehicle.

Two Leopard 2A4s of the 8th batch were taken out of the series as trial samples for the Leopard 2A5 increased fighting value program. The photo shows a Leopard 2A4 (8th batch) of Gebirgspanzerbataillon 8 that bears the yellow maneuver markings of "Blue Force" on its turret. Note the eight smoke dischargers on the side of the turret.

Emblem of
Gebirgspanzerbataillon 8.

14

The last Leopard 2A4s of the 8th batch to be handed over to the German Army were delivered on March 19, 1992 (in a festive manner) to Gebirgspanzerbataillon 8 of Panzerbrigade 12. At the time the German Army had more than 2,125 Leopard 2 battle tanks. This Leopard 2A4 (8th batch) of Gebirgspanzerbataillon 8 wears mud spotted camouflage. The tank's commander is named Spannbauer.

The "Gold Force" units are the lead training troops in the army maneuvers at CMTC Hohenfels. The maneuvers always begin with platoon and company training before all elements of the combat unit combine to attack the "enemy". In this photo the crew members of a Leopard 2A4 (8th batch) platoon prepare themselves for action in the vehicle pool near Albertshofen at the CMTC Hohenfels.

Side view of a Leopard 2A4 (8th batch) of GebPzBtl 8 wearing the red maneuver markings of the "Gold Force" units, as well as yellow angle tactical markings of the company. The rear marker (white ball) shows the tank commander the location of the end of the tank rear, regardless of the turret's position.

A Leopard 2A4 (8th batch) of Gebirgspanzerbataillon 8 of "Blue Force" changes position during the "Schweppermann MILES" maneuver in December 1993 at CMTC Hohenfels. The new steel side aprons are completely assembled on the vehicle. Note that a portion of the rubber padding on the tank tracks that were affixed to the front of the vehicle were exchanged for ice scrapers.

Because of reductions in the German Army in the middle of the 1990s, Gebirgspanzerbataillon 8 was also dissolved. The crew of this Leopard 2A4 (8th batch) of 2nd Company, GebPzBtl 8 has covered the three-color paint scheme with mud. The number "60" on the left leading wheel cover indicates the vehicle's military loading class (weight class), or MLC. To the right is the tactical sign of GebPzBtl 8.

Modern infantry anti-tank weapons are light, mobile, and can destroy a battle tank at 2,000 meters (2,186 yards). If anti-tank teams are deployed in favorable terrain, they can stop entire tank squadrons. The wooded hills at the CMTC Hohenfels are ideally suited for wargame exercises. During the maneuvers of Panzerbataillon 393 of 5.Panzerdivision in December 1995, anti-tank teams and battle tanks work together. Panzerbataillon 393 belongs to the German Army's Schwere Krisenreaktionskräfte Heer (heavy crisis reaction force).

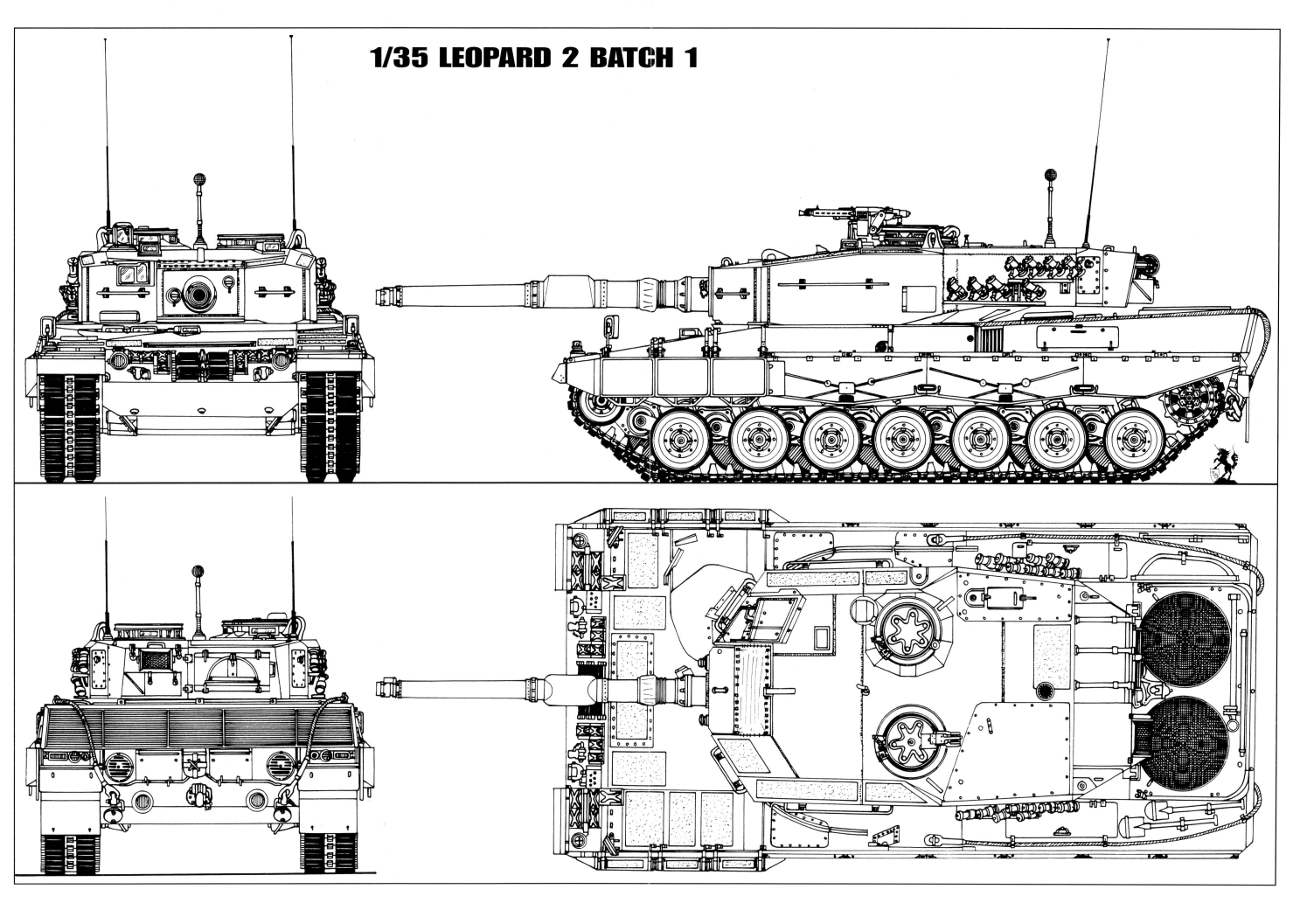

1/35 LEOPARD 2 BATCH 1

Refueling point for a Leopard 2A4 company of PzBtl 214 during the winter exercise in December 1995 at CMTC Hohenfels. The 5-ton MAN 4610 tanker can pump up to 1,200 liters (317 gallons) of diesel fuel into the fuel tank of the Leopard 2. Fuel usage while traveling across the countryside averages about 500 liters per 100 km (132 gallons/62 miles).

An overhead photo of a Leopard 2A4 of PzBtl 214 offers a good view of many details of the new field adjusting system that has been fitted on the mouth of the gun on all Leopard 2 battle tanks in the German Army. Also visible are details of the MILES II training system "Kill Light" and the opened EMES 15. Note that ice scrapers have been assembled on the tank tracks, and the replacement track parts are missing.

The contours of the Leopard 2 are almost indistinguishable through its spotted winter camouflage at a certain distance, as is clearly seen in this photo of two Leopard 2A4 battle tanks of Panzerbataillon 214 at CMTC Hohenfels in December 1995. The lighter front track apron serves to enable the crew to enter and exit more easily.

The CMTC 1-95 maneuver took place under extreme weather and terrain conditions at the exercise area at Hohenfels. First of all, "General Winter" governed things with icy cold winds and a lot of snow, then the weather conditions changed and it began to rain. The resulting mud demanded the utmost from both man and machine, providing exactly the right test conditions for the Leopard 2A4s of Panzerbataillon 104.

The "Bavarian Tiger" insignia of 1st Platoon, 4th Company, Panzerbataillon 104.

Another variation of the winter paint scheme is shown in this photo of a Leopard 2A4 (8th batch) of 4th Company, GebPzBtl 8 during winter maneuvers in January 1995 at CMTC Hohenfels. Here the black spots of the three-color camouflage are painted over with white liquid chalk.

If signals from the laser in the MILES II training system hit the target, the receiver records a hit. Each type of laser has its own code that shows the receiver whether the hit totally cripples or just damages the tank. If an armored fighting vehicle fights a battle tank, no "kill" is possible. A hit is necessary for stopping a battle tank with the anti-tank gun. Some details to be seen on the turret of the Leopard 2 are the Zeiss PERI-R 17 full-view telescopic sights of the commander. In front is the opened EMES 15 range finder and main targeting system of the gunner, with laser range finder, passive low-light-level equipment, and thermal imaging device.

The 2nd platoon of 5th Company, Panzerbataillon 104 has given the name "Thor" to their Leopard 2. Note the radio antenna of the SEM 80/90 radio system as well as part of the MILES II equipment. Leopard 2s from the 5th batch on were fitted with a digital computer for connecting the shooting and dueling simulator. They were also equipped with their own fire suppression system in the turret.

Emblem of Panzerbataillon 104.

A special winter camouflage was used by Panzerbataillon 143 of Panzerbrigade 14 during the "Winterhauch 93" exercise at the Baumholder troop training grounds. Instead of decorating their vehicles with white chalk, the crews covered the large areas on their tanks with white sheets that could be removed if required, depending on the weather situation.

The Leopard 2A4 tanks of the 6th batch, which were produced between 1988 and 1989, featured improved armor plating on the turret and the front of the chassis. Thanks to the new heavy track apron on the front of the chassis introduced in this batch, repairs on the lead wheel can be performed more easily. This "Gold Force" Leopard 2A4 of Panzerlehrbataillon 334 wears the yellow "Wolfsangel" (tactical insignia of Germany's 19.Panzerdivision during World War II) on the turret, as well as the normal red

Before every CMTC Hohenfels rotation, the battalions of the exercising brigades are divided into two combat units (Blue/Gold Force). Each brigade has a reinforced battalion composed of battle tanks, armored personnel carriers, elements of artillery, and field engineers. After completing the combat phase at CMTC Hohenfels, the participating troops are ordered into specified assembly areas, where the next starting point is located. Following each combat phase, separate After Action Review meetings (AAR) are held for both the "Blue Force" and "Gold Force" at platoon, company and battalion levels. This photo shows an AAR of the PzBtl 104 combat unit in December 1995.

The L/44 120mm smoothbore gun of the Leopard 2 basically operates with two types of ammunition. By introducing the 120mm gun into the American M1A1 Abrams, other types of munitions were added. The fire control computer, originally programmed for two types of ammunition, had to be adjusted for these new numbers. This was accomplished with the installation of a digital computer beginning with the 5th batch.

In Army Structure 5 of the German Army, the four combat companies of the tank battalion each have 13 battle tanks (3 tanks in four platoons per company, plus one for the company commander) as well as a battle tank in the company headquarters group. Here we see a platoon of Leopard 2A4s (6th batch) belonging to PzBtl 104 in December 1995. Notice that the front vehicle bears the name of the tank commander on the lower edge of the turret.

During the CMTC Hohenfels rotation there is always a Humvee from the O/C Group (Observer/Controller) with the leading tank of the company. The O/C (umpire) can stop the vehicle or activate it with his "Good Gun" laser pistol.

Assembly area of a platoon of Leopard 2A4 (5th batch) of PzLBtl 93 near Kittensee, CMTC Hohenfels. PzLBtl 93, which was formed in 1956, was equipped with the US M47 battle tank at that time. Later it was the first tank battalion in the German Army to be equipped with the Leopard 2.

The orders given to PzLBtl 93 are principally to carry out training exercises for officers, NCOs and candidates. They are also to test and develop new devices and training techniques, to conduct training exercises in front of high-ranking local and foreign visitors, and to implement training in the defense of the country.

This Leopard 2A4 of PzLBtl 93 belongs to Panzerlehrbrigade 9 stationed in Münster in northern Germany. It is subordinate to the 7.Panzerdivision. PzLBtl 93 is allocated to the main defense force of the German Army.

Help! The commander of this sunken Leopard 2A4 of PzBtl 214 failed to notice a frozen water hole during an attack at CMTC Hohenfels in December 1995. If the superstructure of the battle tank is held by ground suction, only a recovery vehicle can help.

This photo of the sunken Leopard 2A4 of PzBtl 214 provides a good look at some of the details of the turret roof fitted with the MILES II training system. The battle vehicles that are fitted with the MILES II training system also have a Global Position System (GPS) and a transmitter that makes each vehicle moving in the troop training area visible on a computer screen in the control room. This tells which vehicles have shot at which targets.

"Road markings" of Panzerbrigade 21 and Panzerlehrbrigade 9 with tactical insignia for the tank troops, typical for the German Army in April 1996 near Hohenfels.

This Leopard 2A4 of PzBtl 214 of Panzerbrigade 21, 7.Panzerdivision is part of the German Army's heavy crisis reaction force. The battalion's insignia, the "Lippische Rose", is clearly visible on the turret near the EMES 15. In 1997 PzBtl 214 was re-equipped with the Leopard 2A5 KWS II.

Commander emblem of Panzerbrigade 21, part of the German heavy crisis reaction force.

PzBtl 33, which also belongs to the heavy crisis reaction force, is fitted out with the Leopard 2A4 here. The insignia of PzBtl 33 is a yellow African palm on a black/white background, seen here on the right side of the turret. In 1996, PzBtl 33 was the first unit to be equipped with the Leopard 2A5, and newly outfitted for combat.

Emblem of
Panzerbataillon 154,
Panzerbrigade 34, 5 (GE)
Panzerdivision, equipped
with Leopard 2A4.

The waste of material at CMTC Hohenfels is quite considerable during the exercises. This Leopard 2A4 of PzBtl 154, Panzerbrigade 34 had a whole leading wheel torn away by a rock.

Leopard 2A3, batch 4, Panzerbataillon 123, Panzerbrigade 12, "Royal Sword 90" maneuver, Sulzbach-Rosenberg, October 1990

The tactical number on the turret identifies this Leopard 2A3 as the 3rd vehicle of 2nd Platoon, 2nd Company. The new Leopard 2A5 battalions of the German Army have discarded the turret numbers. The battalion insignia of Panzerbataillon 123, the yellow "Knight's helmet", is painted on the left front side of the turret. As from batch 4 onward, all Leopard 2 battle tanks were delivered from the factory with the new three-color camouflage. The orange light on the turret roof is switched on during convoys on public roads.

Leopard 2A4, batch 7, Panzerbataillon 214, 7.Panzerdivision, CMTC Hohenfels, December 1995

The crew of this Leopard 2A4 has the black patches of the three-color camouflage painted over with white chalk during the winter maneuver in December 1995 at CMTC Hohenfels. The yellow "wolf's angel" above the smoke dischargers identifies this vehicle as part of the "Blue Force" and was the tactical insignia of the 19.Panzerdivision during the Russian campaign in WWII. The side skirts are removed during maneuvers in Hohenfels to prevent unnecessary damages to the chassis. The importance of the blue number "93" on the turret front is not known. The large box on the turret roof in which the personal belongings of the crew are stored is unusual.

Leopard 2A4, 41 (NL) Tankbataljon, 41 (NL) Lichte Brigade, "Light Viper 93" maneuver, Weser-Emsland, June 1993

Only the 41 (NL) Tankbataljon carries the "Black lion with sword" emblem on the turret. The white "GE" on black background indicates Dutch unit stationed in Germany. The MILES training system is fixed to the green velcro band on the turret during training. The tent tarpaulin serves to camouflage the chassis. Other outer alterations are the FN-MAG machine gun, the long radio antenna, and only six smoke dischargers on each side of the turret. All Dutch Leopard 2s, including the A4 version, were delivered from the factory in olive green color.

Leopard 2A5 KWS II, Panzerbataillon 33, 7.Panzerdivision, CMTC Hohenfels, April 1997

This vehicle belongs to the 2nd Company of Panzerbataillon 33 and is seen fitted with the SAWE-RF/MILES II Training System during the "CMTC Rotation" in April 1997 at the US 7th Army training center in Hohenfels. The side skirts and the extra turret baskets were removed before the actual exercise. On the rear of the turret is the simplified shape of the battalion insignia of Panzerbataillon 33, a yellow "palm tree", whose origins dates back to Rommel's Afrika Korps. The former ammunition hatch on the turret below the national cross has been deleted in a previous efficiency upgrading measure.

Because of the political situation in the world after the fall of the Berlin wall, CAT was arranged for the CENTAG army group for the last time in 1991 at the American troop training area at Grafenwöhr. Here a Leopard 2A4 of PzBtl 153 of the CENTAG team drives back to its original position following the "battle run". PzBtl 153, which is one of the oldest tank battalions in the German Army, was refitted with the Leopard battle tank in 1985. The name on the turret is an allusion to the well-known motion picture from the early '90s.

The Canadian Army Trophy (CAT) was a NATO tank shooting competition waged between the teams of the army groups NORTAG and CENTAG. This photo shows a Dutch Leopard 2A4 platoon of 43 (NL) Tankbataljon (NORTHAG) during the "battle run" on range 301 at the Grafenwöhr Training Area during CAT 91. In each "battle run" the unit fires at fixed and movable targets both from fixed positions and while underway.

There are 32 targets and machine-gun squads ready for use by each unit during the CAT. Standing tanks can fire at targets at a range of 2,000 meters (2,186 yards) and moving battle vehicles can shoot from up to 1,200 meters (1,412 yards) away. Note the Dutch national flag on the rear of the vehicle in the photo, as well as the lettering "CAT 1991" on the right side of the turret of the Leopard 2A4 of 43 (NL) Tankbataljon.

The image of a tiger's head was often used in connection with the CAT competition and often decorated the tanks of the participating teams, as is the case with this Leopard 2A4 of PzBtl 84 of the NORTAG team. Panzerbataillon 84 was formed in 1959. In 1981 it became one of the first units to receive the Leopard 2 battle tank. During CAT 75 the Panzerbataillon 84 won first prize while equipped with the Leopard 1 battle tank.

The CAT 89 competition turned out to be a very close race right up to the end. The day before it ended, 1st platoon of 4th Company, PzBtl 203, seen in this photo, was a favorite. However, the German team was beaten by the Dutch Leopard 2s of 41 (NL) Tankbataljon, which shot very well.

During CAT 89 the Leopard 2 platoon of PzBtl 203 won second place with 17,735 points. The first place awards in CAT 89 were all won by Leopard 2 teams, which illustrates once again the impressive output of that weapons system. Note the German national flag on the 120mm gun barrel of the Leopard 2 of PzBtl 203.

As the first unit of the heavy crisis reaction force in the German Bundeswehr, Panzerbataillon 33 from Luttermersen received the new Leopard 2A5 in the stage II improved battle version. This photo shows a Leopard 2A5 KWS II of 2nd Company, PzBtl 33 during the first maneuver in CMTC Hohenfels in April 1997.

In the spring of 1992 the three user states, Germany, the Netherlands and Switzerland, decided to refit the Leopard 2 to the KWS stage II. The KWS stage II sets the standard for better armor plating through exchangeable extra armor on the turret. It also features measures for improving fire control and command and control.

The side segments of the extra armor can be folded away. On the left side of the turret there is an internal housing for storing the cleaning equipment for the gun.

A view of the left side of a Leopard 2A5 KWS II shows the driving lights and horn, towing hooks, snow grousers, and replacement track parts on the front of the tank's hull. Behind them, on the turret turning ring, are the empty holders for the twelve camouflage net poles. During maneuvers with the MILES II training system, the gun illustration device (Hoffmann Device) is attached to the left side.

A close-up view of the reinforced roof of the turret. Behind the extra armor of the turret front, the EMES 15 main target telescopic sights help to observe, measure range, and direct the fire of the guns on board. A thermal imaging device is built into the EMES 15. To the left of this is the FERO auxiliary telescopic sights of the gunner, which can take over for the main gun and the Blenden machine gun if the fire control system breaks down.

The attachment of extra armor to the front of the turret also provides the driver with better protection against fire from above. The driver's hatch was completely redesigned to allow it to be moved horizontally in one motion. Two angled mirrors are fitted to the hatch, and a third is installed at the left front of the tank's superstructure.

A top view of the turret of a Leopard 2A5 KWS II shows the assistant gunner's hatch with the mounting for the anti-aircraft machine gun. Between the assistant gunner's hatch and the commander's hatch is the CFK-Light ("Kill Light") of the MILES II training system.

The highest point of the Leopard 2A5 KWS II is the PERI-R 17 panoramic view periscope that is now fitted behind the commander's hatch because of the extra armor on the turret. The rotating part of the device allows the commander to make 360-degree observations that assist him to target reconnaissance, provide target information in his orders to the gunner and supervise the battle tank. The antenna in the middle belongs to the MILES II training system.

The installation of a reverse gear driving aid, which consists of a camera on the rear of the vehicle and a TV screen in the driver's area, is one of the new implementations on the chassis of the Leopard 2A5 KWS II. The reverse driving camera, which is fixed to the rear of the vehicle above the radiator exhaust grating on the rear of the hull, enables the driver to drive backwards under combat conditions (with a closed hatch). The red devil is the insignia of the 1st platoon of 2nd Company and the yellow African palm to the right and left of the turret is the battalion insignia of PzBtl 33.

The most recognizable external characteristic of the new Leopard 2A5 KWS II is the wedge-shaped extra armor on the shield and front of the turret. The so-called attachment modules are easily changeable and can be refitted to all existing Leopard 2 superstructures and turrets.

With the turret position at 11 o'clock, the driver can operate the Leopard 2A5 KWS II with an open hatch and look outside while driving.

The "Shark" platoon insignia of 3rd Company, Panzerbataillon 33, painted at the turret front side.

The Leopard 2A5 KWS II, such as the one shown here photographed at Bergen-Hohne in November 1997, is fitted with a storage box at the rear of the turret and two bins on each side of it. The rear box is large enough to contain rain protection, the crew's personal equipment, cable drums, vehicle covers and water canisters. The shark on the turret basket of this Leopard is the unit insignia of Panzerbataillon 3/33.

This side view allows the strength of the new additional armor to be seen. Sharp attachment modules reach almost to the bore evacuator of the 120mm gun. Because of its shape, the Leopard 2A5 KWS II is also known as "the shrew".

The extra armor on the right side of the turret is removable. Visible on the inside of the extra armor on the right is the deep-water snorkel assembly used for fording water.

Overall view of the huge turret housing of the Leopard 2A5 KWS II with all new fittings. The refitted Leopard 2A5 remains within the prescribed combat weight of 62.5 tonnes. Carrying a crew of four and full of fuel, the A5 version reaches a total weight of 60.5 tonnes. The turret bins attached to the right and left rear of the turret had been removed before the exercise started.

This view of the superstructure and turret housing of the Leopard 2A5 KWS II shows to advantage the strength of the side armor. Note the sliding driver's hatch.

The yellow "Afrika Korps" palm, emblem of Panzerbataillon 33, Panzerbrigade 21, 7 (GE) Panzerdivision, equipped with Leopard 2A5 KWS II.

Battalion crest of Panzerbataillon 33 shows a yellow African palm tree against a black/white Prussian background color. This crest is applied to all Leopard 2A5 KWS II of Panzerbataillon 33.

Leopard 2A5 KWS II of 2nd Company, PzBtl 33 in the assembly area of the training village at CMTC Hohenfels, April 1997. The number "70" on the right leading track cover gives the military load class in metric tons. Next to this is the squadron insignia, which has its origins with Rommel's Afrika Korps. The tactical insignia is located on the left leading track cover.

Unlucky tank! During the spring maneuver of 1997 at CMTC Hohenfels, obviously through a driver's error, a Leopard 2A5 KWS II of Panzerbataillon 33 slipped down an embankment and partially buried itself. Because of the condition of the soil the tank could not free itself. A Bergepanzer 3 Büffel armored recovery vehicle eventually freed the Leopard from its unlucky position.

The whole of 2nd Company, Panzerbataillon 33, which fields thirteen Leopard 2A5 KWS II tanks, prepares for exercises on a village street in Enselwange in April 1997 at CMTC Hohenfels. The exercise begins with orders being given to the training battalions, which then take up their initial positions.

Seen here in a parade during the spring exercise in April 1997 at CMTC Hohenfels is 2nd Company, Panzerbataillon 33, which is supported by Marder 1A3 APC of Panzergrenadierbataillon 212. The battle exercises of the Leopard 2 tank battalions at the CMTC are divided into individual training phases that combined to make a complete tactical situation.

The dual combat field simulation using the MILES II training system is the most modern method of combat training available today. The MILES training system has a passive aspect that employs sensors to show the hits that are taken and an active side that uses lasers to indicate the effects of the weapons. Since 1993 the German Army has used this qualified training method increasingly for its heavy crisis reaction forces.

The German Army will refit 225 of their Leopard 2s with the A5 KWS II variant. This will mean that the tank battalions of the heavy crisis reaction forces and the Eurocorps will be fitted out first. Seen in this photo is a Leopard 2A5 KWS II of PzBtl 3/33 at Bergen-Hohne in November 1997.

Before the Leopard 2A5 KWS II was introduced to the German tank troops, there were long years of work testing individual measures for increasing the combat efficiency in troop trials. This Leopard 2A5 KWS II that belongs to Panzerbataillon 33 is seen here in November 1997 at Bergen-Hohne.

The increase in the need for combat efficiency in the Leopard 2A5 KWS II is partly attributable to the deadly hand-held, guided anti-tank weapons that are always being improved, as well as the threat from above from combat helicopters and ground-assault aircraft. Because the MILAN guided anti-tank weapon used by German tank grenadiers (infantry) is incompatible with the MILES II training system, the German Army uses the American Dragon in exercises at Hohenfels.

With the exception of the tank commander, the four-man crew of the Leopard 2A5 KWS II is entirely composed of conscripted men who, after their initial basic training, receive special training that begins with driving, firing and loading. A large part of the training is carried out using shooting simulators.

During training the Leopard 2 crew members familiarize themselves with the use of various types of ammunition by firing the gun with training munitions. The ultimate goal of the training is the mastery of combat firing within the scope of the unit.

Once they have been trained to fire their tank's gun, the Leopard crew has become a team. The last stage of training, undergoing combat exercises, then follows. In these exercises cooperation with other types of troops, such as the panzer grenadiers (mechanized infantry), is practiced.

The weapon hydraulics were replaced by a fully electronic system in the turret of the Leopard 2A5 KWS II. Not only does it save space inside, but the fire hazard posed by escaping hydraulic oil is also reduced.

Tanks from 2nd Company, PzBtl 33 are loaded onto German Railways rail cars at the railway station of Parsberg after completing the spring maneuvers of 1997 at CMTC Hohenfels. (R. Hochstatter)

The commander of Panzerbataillon 33 leads a counterattack with his Leopard 2A5 KWS II at the front line near Kittensee, CMTC Hohenfels, in January 1998 during the maneuver "Harte Faust 98". The commander's tank is distinguished by the red/black battalion flag (Bataillonsstandarde) with the white numeral "33" on the right side of the turret. The MLC-marking and the battalion crest are visible on the right chain guard. The red maneuver cross is the symbol of the "Gold Force" (Übungstruppe Gold) maneuver troops.

Leopard 2A5 KWS II of 3rd Company, Panzerbataillon 33 of the "Gold Force" during battle near Kittensee, CMTC Hohenfels in January 1998. The brand-new Leopard 2A5 KWS II are covered with an icy mud coat; the lateral turret storage bins are missing. The "Yellow Palm Tree" at the turret rear is the symbol of the Gefechtsverband 33 (Task Force 33) during the maneuver "Harte Faust 98", the markings "C II" and the "bear head" are tactical platoon markings.

The Panzerbataillon 393 is the third tank battalion in the heavy KRK (Krisenreaktionskräfte) of the Bundeswehr to be issued their first new Leopard 2A5 KWS II in mid-1997. The photograph shows a rear view of a tank in 3rd Company, PzBtl 393 employed at the forward defense lines. The vertical "Yellow Arrow" at the turret storage bin and side identifies the "Blue Force", here the "Gefechtsverband 393" during the "Harte Faust 98" maneuver at CMTC Hohenfels in January 1998. The two wheel chocks fastened at the turret rear are used for securing the tank during railroad transport. The tank crew secures the vehicle with the barbed wire in nighttime.

The crew of 3rd Company, PzBtl 33 is preparing its Leopard 2A5 KWS II for railroad transport after winter maneuvers in Hohenfels at the Parsberg railway station on a frosty afternoon in February 1998. The black camouflage spots are painted over with whitewash. The winter camouflage at the tank hull is covered with mud. The metal aprons were mounted only shortly before the road transport from Hohenfels to Parsberg loading station.

This train behind the German flag is ready to transport Leopard 2A5 KWS II of Panzerbataillon 214, Panzerbrigade 21, 7.Panzerdivision to their home base in Augustdorf. The tanks feature the "Gold Force" maneuver marking; differing versions of the winter camouflage were applied to the new Leopard 2A5 KWS II for the first time during the maneuver in CMTC Hohenfels.

A somewhat unusual portrait of a Leopard 2A5 KWS II battle tank. Panzerhauptmann Alme of 3rd Company, PzBtl 393, 5.Panzerdivision is photographed with a visiting officer from Mali, Africa uniformed as a German Army officer during the maneuver CMTC 4-98 in Hohenfels, April 1998. The German Army is frequently host to a number of foreign military personnel from non-NATO countries who are familiarized with tactics and equipment of the German tank troops.

Maneuvers on difficult terrain at the CMTC Hohenfels deliver a severe strain on tanks and material. This Leopard 2A5 KWS II of PzBtl 33 is broken down and raised the yellow flag. Following inspection of the damage, the crew of the Bergepanzer 3 Büffel ARV summoned to the scene decides to tow the disabled tank away.

The Bergepanzer 3 Büffel ARV was developed to operate in with the fast Leopard 2 battle tank. While the Bergepanzer has lifted the heavy engine cover plate, the crew of the Leopard 2A5 KWS II of PzBtl 214, Panzerbrigade 21 removes the engine connections. The lateral steel turret reinforcement is disengaged. Removing the entire Leopard 2 engine block is accomplished in very short time.

A closer look at the damage to the broken-down Leopard 2A5 KWS II of 2nd Company, PzBtl 33. During a simulated attack, the commander of the tank failed to see a bump on the ground, the speeding tank was thrown several meters into the air, and torn off the front idler on hard landing. This will require several hours of hard work for the repair. The white triangle (NATO-cross) between the tactical signs facilitates orientation to the forward vehicle during nighttime operations.

After removing the engine cover plate, one can get a full view of the engine compartment of a Leopard 2A5 KWS II with all details of the MTU MB 873 ka-501 engine. Note the two large round air filters of the 12-cylinder 47.6 liter turbo-charged diesel engine.

During live fire exercise of 5th Company, PzBtl 393 on the Live Fire Range 6 (Schießbahn 6) in May 1998 in Bergen-Hohne, the crew of a Leopard 2A5 KWS II is loading 120mm armor-piercing ammunition. A special version of this KE munitions was successfully employed in 1991 during the Gulf War in American M1A1 Abrams tanks and was dubbed "Silver Bullet".

The Future: Leopard 2A5 KWS II

Beginning in the year 2000 the combat stage (KWS I) upgrade is to be carried out on the Leopard 2A5 KWS II. The KWS stage includes another increase in the firepower through a longer gun barrel called the 120 L/55. (A. Kirchhoff)

The firepower of the 120mm gun can be considerably increased by lengthening the barrel from .44 caliber length to .55 caliber length and using the more powerful KE ammunition (LKE II). The armor-piercing capacity will then be almost doubled compared to the capacity at the beginning of the '80s. The new LKE II ammunition for the Leopard 2A5 is to be introduced with the KWS I. But thanks to the 4,000-meter (4,372-yard) maximum range of the old fire control computer, the gun's range will not be increased. (A. Kirchhoff)

Euro-Leopard 2

The Swiss Army has bought a total of 380 Leopard 87 tanks that feature the A4 outfit. The Leopard 87 tank is equipped with a US vehicle radio outfit, built in Switzerland under license, as well as the Swiss MG 87. It also features additional attachments for ten more snow grousers. (A. Kirchhoff)

Another characteristic that distinguishes the Swiss Leopard 87 tank from the German version is the removable exhaust silencer (for reducing noise) that is attached to the rear of the vehicle on all Swiss Army Leopard tanks. Immediately in front of the smoke discharger system on both sides of the turret are two holders for cooling hot machine gun barrels. An external intercom is attached to the rear of the turret. (A. Kirchhoff)

A Dutch Leopard 2A4 of 42 (NL) Tankbataljon in the forward base of Alpha team in Novi Travnik, Bosnia-Herzegovina in September 1996. The IFOR insignia was applied in white lettering below the name of the tank ("Acrid") on both sides of the turret. The Dutch IFOR troops used the Leopard 2 battle tank for securing their checkpoints.

Altogether there were six Dutch Leopard 2A4s and a "Bergingstanks 600 KN Büffel" armored recovery vehicle stationed at the forward base of Alpha team of the Dutch IFOR contingent. The vehicles stood in the open with covers over them, though repair and maintenance work was carried out in tents.

In 1996 the Dutch Army received the last of a total of 445 Leopard 2 battle tanks. The Leopard 2s of the Dutch Army are the same as batches 2 and 3 of the German Army. Externally the Dutch Leopard 2 can be recognized by the six smoke dischargers on each side. This photo shows a Dutch Leopard 2A4 of 104.verkenningsebataljon (Tank Reconnaissance Battalion) during the battle exercise "Light Viper 93". The tent covers on the side aprons serve to camouflage the chassis.

The Dutch forces place great value in having Leopard 2s that are similar to the German ones. The maintenance of the Leopard 2 weapons system is less expensive this way, making them more economical for the future. Seen here is a photo of a Dutch Leopard 2A4 of 101 (NL) Tankbataljon and a German Leopard 2A4 of Panzerbataillon 24 during the exercise "Active Sword 97" near Barme/Weser. Both units are subordinate to the new German/Dutch Corps.

The external alterations on the Dutch Leopard 2, compared to the German type, lie principally in the turret area: the turret and anti-aircraft FN MG, the radio installation and the enhanced driver's optical equipment are of Dutch production, as are the six smoke dischargers on each side of the turret. The lion with sword, the emblem of the Dutch forces, was only worn by 41 (NL) Tankbataljon. This photograph shows a Dutch Leopard 2A4 of 41 (NL) Tankbataljon in the "Light Viper" maneuver near Hoya.

In 1984, 41 (NL) Tankbataljon was equipped with the Leopard 2, but in 1994 the battalion was dissolved. Because of the reduction in the number of forces in the Dutch Army, 114 Leopard 2A4s were sold to Austria. This Leopard 2A4 of 41 (NL) Tankbataljon was photographed during the "Light Viper" maneuver near Hoya.

This is a NL Leopard 2A4 of 41 (NL) Tankbataljon seen during the "Light Viper" maneuver of the restructured 41 (NL) Lichte Brigade. After the 1st NL Corps was dissolved, the remaining Dutch units were integrated into the newly formed German/Dutch Corps.

Emblem of 41 (NL) Lichte Brigade during exercise "Light Viper 93".

Cold War scenario: Mi-24 Hind attack helicopters engage in combat with a Dutch Leopard 2A4 of the 11 (NL) Tankbataljon. Yesterday's enemy is now a welcomed participant in the "Rhino Drawsko 97" maneuvers. This impressive photo was taken during the first maneuver with the Dutch Army on the Polish troop training ground at Drawsko Pommerski in April 1997.

During the Dutch Army's "Rhino Drawsko 97" maneuver in Poland, 30 Leopard 2A4 battle tanks of 11 (NL) Tankbataljon were transported by ship to Stettin in Poland, and then by rail to the training ground. Note the American MILES training equipment on the turret of the Dutch Leopard 2A4, as well as the olive-green camouflage paint scheme. The tactical insignia was covered over.

Dutch Leopard 2A4 of 11 (NL) Tankbataljon at a refueling station on the Polish training ground at Drawsko Pommerski in April 1997. Every Dutch tank squadron has fourteen tanks: the commander and his deputy each have a tank at their disposal, and three platoons each composed of four tanks.

In May 1996 the first Leopard 2A5 KWS IIs were handed over to the Dutch Army. Other conspicuous external differences from the German version are the larger holders for the wedges on the rear of the turret, as well as the lighter rear track apron. The Dutch version has a 7.62mm MG made by the Belgian firm FN as its anti-aircraft machine gun. A French type FM-9000 vehicle radio is installed in the inside of the Leopard 2A5 KWS II.

The improved, powerful KE ammunition DM-33 can also be fired from the L/44 120mm smoothbore gun, the standard gun of the Leopard 2. At the end of 1999 the Royal Dutch Army plans to equip 11 (NL) Tankbataljon with a modified version of this tank, the Leopard 2A5 KWS II. In this photo a Leopard 2A4 NL of 11 (NL) Tankbataljon participates in the "Rhino Drawsko" maneuver in April 1997. Observe the Dutch vehicle number and the weight class (MLC) on the front of the vehicle.

Dutch Leopard 2A5 KWS II of A Company, 42 (NL) Tankbataljon during the first "Active Sword" maneuver of the new German/Dutch Corps on the troop training ground at Bergen-Hohne in October 1997. The Dutch version of the Leopard 2A5 KWS II differs externally from the German version by having six smoke dischargers on each side of the turret, as well as by having a thicker and longer antenna (not assembled on this vehicle). This vehicle of A Company bears the word "Assassin" on the side of the turret.

A Leopard 2A5 KWS II of 42 (NL) Tankbataljon in high speed during maneuvers in April 1998 near Zootkamp in the Netherlands. The Royal Dutch Army adopted the German tri-color camouflage of bronze-green (RAL 6031), leather-brown (RAL 8027) and tar-black (RAL 9021) for its new Leopard 2A5 KWS II. The MLC marking "70" on the right side of the tank hull is in gray, numerals are in white.

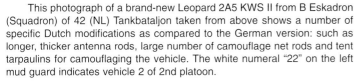

This photograph of a brand-new Leopard 2A5 KWS II from B Eskadron (Squadron) of 42 (NL) Tankbataljon taken from above shows a number of specific Dutch modifications as compared to the German version: such as longer, thicker antenna rods, large number of camouflage net rods and tent tarpaulins for camouflaging the vehicle. The white numeral "22" on the left mud guard indicates vehicle 2 of 2nd platoon.

"Massive Steel". Another Leopard 2A5 KWS II from B Eskadron (Squadron) of 42 (NL) Tankbataljon with turret facing near. Note the larger version of mounts for the wheel chocks at the turret rear. The rear storage bin holds the camouflage nets. The aluminum box is lacquered in original camouflage color and is mounted in identical position at the turret roof of each vehicle in this unit. The Dutch national emblems and platoon number are affixed to the left front mud guard, the right front mud guard features the tactical signs.

The Swedish version of the Leopard 2A5, which is named "Stridsvagn 122", differs greatly from the German/Dutch versions of the Mannheimer configuration. It features significantly larger extra armor on the turret roof and the front hull area, as well as halogen lamps. The Stridsvagn 122 weighs 62 tonnes. The German Bundeswehr originally planned to buy the Leopard 2A5 in the Stridsvagn 122 version, but had to abandon this plan due to a lack of funds. (A. Kirchhoff)

The Swedish tank brigades are to receive a total of 210 vehicles in the Stridsvagn 122 version. The turret roof on the Stridsvagn 122 has been strengthened with additional protection. The tank is also equipped with a command and control system with the following properties: transfer of orders and information, assessment of the situation, local mapping, orientation in the countryside, target identification, as well as RAMAN lasers, which are safe for the eyes. (A. Kirchhoff)

Leopard Armored Recovery Vehicle

From the introduction of the Leopard 2 until 1992, the Bergepanzer 2, built on the basis of the Leopard 1, was the standard recovery vehicle of the German tank troops and the Leopard 2 tank battalions. The Bergepanzer 2 Standard ARV (Armored Recovery Vehicle) has a combat weight of only 40.6 tonnes, while the weight of the Leopard 2 is 55 tonnes. In difficult terrain and for longer street marches, there are usually two Bergepanzer 2 Standard ARVs used. They may be seen in this photo of PzBtl 363 at the "Fraenkisher Schild" army exercises in 1986.

"Obelix" is a comic character, representing strong and powerful. This figure is painted on the crane of a Bergepanzer 3 Büffel armored recovery vehicle of Panzerbataillon 393, Hohenfels, January 1996.

Bergepanzer 3 Büffel (buffalo) ARV, is an up-rated development on the chassis of the Leopard 2 battle tank. The German Army received their first Büffel in August 1992. So far 100 Bergepanzer 3 Büffel armored recovery vehicles have been ordered, and there is an option for another 75 vehicles. The photo shows a Büffel belonging to PzBtl 393 in January 1996 at CMTC Hohenfels. Note the lack of track aprons.

With the Bergepanzer 3 Büffel ARV, the tank troops have a supporting vehicle that considerably improves the fighting ability of the Leopard 2 battle tank. The weight of the Büffel is 54.5 tonnes, and its main winch installation has a total length of 180 meters (197 yards). This photo shows the recovering of a Leopard 2A4 by a Büffel of PzBtl 104 at CMTC Hohenfels in December 1993.

Having the recovery equipment of the Bergepanzer 3 Büffel armored recovery vehicle located above the plow blade allows the three-man crew to perform recovering tasks under protection of the tank so no crew member has to leave the vehicle. Seen here is a Büffel of GebPzBtl 8 in winter camouflage in January 1995 at CMTC Hohenfels.

A tank train. Here, during the "Rhino Drawsko" maneuver in April 1997 in Poland, a Dutch "Bergingstank 600 KN Büffel" tows two broken down vehicles at the same time: a Leopard 2A4 and a YPR 765 PRI armored personnel carrier. Many of the components of the Bergepanzer 3 Büffel originate from the Leopard 2 battle tank. From a distance of one meter (about a yard) the crane boom can lift 30 tonnes.

The Bergepanzer 3 Büffel armored recovery vehicle was developed and purchased jointly by Germany and the Netherlands. In 1992 the first "Bergingstank 600 KN Büffel" was delivered to the Dutch Army. This photo shows the 54.5-tonne Büffel of 104 (NL) Tankbataljon towing a broken down Leopard 2 battle tank over a Ribbon Bridge near Eystrup on the Weser river during the "Light Viper 93" maneuver.